THIS THING CALLED KINDERGARTEN

By Dolly Venables

Illustrations by Stephen Riggins

LANDON
HAIL
PRESS

Text and illustrations copyright © 2023 Dolly Venables

Published by Landon Hail Press

Paperback ISBN: 978-1-959955-28-3

Hardback ISBN: 978-1-959955-29-0

This book is dedicated to the late
Diane M. Swisher, an amazing, highly regarded
kindergarten teacher in the Huron,
South Dakota School District.
Her genuine love for each and every child she
taught changed lives, one student at a time.
You truly made a difference, Diane.
Gone too soon, you are missed.

Dear Friends,

Whether you're young or older, doing something for the first time can be frightening. The fear of the unknown, not knowing what to expect, can cause huge butterflies to take flight in our tummies.

That's when we rely on those around us, our friends, family, loved ones, and teachers, for support and encouragement. These are powerful tools we can use when we're attempting to help someone through an uncertain time. Positive reinforcement is key to building a person's confidence, and with confidence and solid self-esteem, we can conquer any challenge.

My hope for *This Thing Called Kindergarten* is that each and every little person starting kindergarten will know how smart, strong, and capable of success they are from the support, encouragement, and praise they receive at home, from loved ones, and from their teacher.

    With love,

Dolly Venables

P.S. For those days when you don't feel like you can conquer the challenge, I've written a special "Positivity Poem" just for you. My prayer is that it provides you with the positivity, strength, and confidence you need to accomplish anything! Scan the QR Code below for a positive boost that will get your day off to a perfect start. May it lift your spirits and remind you how awesome you are! You've got this!

"Rise and shine," says Mama. "You don't want to be late. It's your first day of kindergarten and it's going to be great!"

Annie groans her best groan and sighs her best sigh, and try as she might, she cannot figure out why.

Why she has to get up so early, why she has to go to school.

Is it really that necessary? Is it really that cool?

Annie plays well with others. She is funny, sweet, and smart.

The problem with going to kindergarten is that Annie and her mama are going to be apart.

 Annie loves being close to her mother. Her mama makes her feel strong.

 What if she goes to kindergarten and everything there goes wrong?

Annie just wants to stay at home, snuggle with Mama, and ride her bike.

After all, this seems like a perfect day for them to go on a hike!

Annie thinks and thinks, but she cannot come up with a single reason.

Why she has to go to kindergarten this or any other season!

Mama hugs Annie tight and strokes her beautiful, long, blonde curls.

She tells her about the wonderful things she'll do at school and how she'll meet lots of boys and girls.

Annie begs to stay at home, but Mama assures her she'll be fine.

"I promise you'll love kindergarten, Annie. You're going to have a great time!"

"I'm so proud of you, sweetheart. You're going to be a star.

You'll be a super student, and I know you'll go far."

"You're a brilliant little girl, Annie, and I'll just bet,

You'll be the teacher's helper, and you'll be the teacher's pet!"

"So, while you're at kindergarten, Annie, and we are apart,

Remember I love you and you are always in my heart."

"Now, let's get you ready, so you can be on your way.

For the first day of kindergarten is such a very special day!"

Mama dresses her up all fancy, like those rich English queens.

Good grief! Holy cow! All Annie wants is her jeans.

Mama tells her a good breakfast will help to make her smart.

But pancakes, cereal, fruit, toast, milk, and juice *all* at once? Annie nearly bursts apart!

The bus ride is just awful—bouncy, bumpy, long, and loud.

Annie wouldn't have considered this thing called kindergarten had she known there'd be such a crowd!

The place called school is really huge. How will she find her way?

Oh me, oh my, oh why, oh why didn't Annie just stay home and play?

A lady named Debbie takes Annie to her class. It's not hard to find at all.

Through the door, to the left, it's the room at the end of the hall.

It is time to meet her teacher. She is waiting in the room.

Ohhhh, what if she's grumpy? What if she's grouchy? What if she rides a broom!

Well, she isn't grouchy, and she isn't grumpy. She is as nice as she could be.

She says she'll teach Annie colors and help her count past three!

She says she'll learn her ABCs and maybe play a game.

She'll go for walks and play with blocks. Mrs. Swisher is her name.

She reads an awesome story about a delicious gingerbread man.

Then the class bakes a cake like the one in the book, where he jumps right out of the pan!

They search the whole school high and low, and he puts up quite a fight!

But when at last they find him, they eat every little bite! Yum!

They go outside for recess, and Annie can't believe her eyes.

There are swings and slides and merry-go-rounds in every color, shape, and size!

Annie quickly realizes that Mama had been right.

She *is* loving kindergarten and shouldn't have put up such a fight.

Annie meets a blue-eyed girl named Betsy. They become the best of friends.

They play and laugh and learn together. She hopes it never ends!

The months fly by, with all the cutting, pasting, and drawing to do.

Halloween is here before they know it, and Mrs. Swisher sings a song called "Witches Brew."

Next comes Thanksgiving, then Christmas with parties galore.

With wiggly, giggly excitement, Annie wants more, more, more.

Every day at school is special. Kindergarten is the place to be.

Annie's excited to tell Mama all about it and share the things she gets to see.

Each day, when school is over, Annie feels a little sad.

After all, this thing called kindergarten is not half bad!

She can't wait until tomorrow. She won't be a minute late.

Because, you see, *ANNIE LOVES KINDERGARTEN.*

IT IS GREAT!

Honoring Mrs. Swisher

This Thing Called Kindergarten is a story that comes from Dolly's heart. Having had the opportunity to work with a truly remarkable kindergarten teacher by the name of Diane Swisher, Dolly witnessed every day Mrs. Swisher's patience and love for each student.

She dedicated her life to teaching the children beyond academics. She instilled in them that they were important and they were special. Those first-day tears and fears dissipated quickly, as the children realized this kindergarten classroom was a safe place with a kind, caring teacher who would always be there for them.

Mrs. Swisher passed away November 8, 2009 at the age of sixty-three, after sharing thirty-one years of her life teaching in Huron. Diane may be gone, but she is not forgotten. Her name comes up frequently in conversations with former students. What a great teacher she was. How much her students learned from her and loved her, how gentle, genuine, and kind she was, and how she still impacts their lives today.

This one's for you, Diane. May your legacy live on through this book. You are a true legend. My hope for all little people starting kindergarten is that they are fortunate enough to have a teacher just like you, so they can't wait to go back to school the very next day!

About Dolly Venables

Dolly Venables is a first-time author who makes her writing debut with *This Thing Called Kindergarten.* She grew up in the Black Hills of South Dakota before moving to the eastern part of the state, Huron, in 1979, where she still resides with her husband, Gary. For several years, Dolly was employed at Washington Elementary School, where she had the opportunity to work with a phenomenal kindergarten teacher named Diane Swisher.

Diane inspired Dolly to love and nurture the students and help them realize their full potential. That experience, along with Dolly's love for writing, motivated her to write this book, so students everywhere would know that kindergarten will be an unbelievable year of their life, one they will never forget.

About Stephen Riggins

After a stint playing bass in a punk band, Stephen began his career as a graphic designer, eventually working his way up to vice president in the experiential design and advertising industry and then, to Chief Marketing Officer of an international development agency. Currently, Stephen is an illustrator, designer, and educator who draws and creates things on his family farm somewhere in the American Midwest.

Printed in the USA
CPSIA information can be obtained
at www.ICGtesting.com
LVHW060941191223
766780LV00017B/378